The Peace Manual

With
appreciation
for your skill
and caring,

The Peace Manual

A GUIDE TO PERSONAL-POLITICAL INTEGRATION

By Frank Rubenfeld, Ph.D.

Published by: Lion-Lamb Press
               678 Santa Rosa Avenue
               Berkeley, California 94707

ISBN: 0-9616424-0-8

Printed in the United States of America

10   9   8   7   6   5   4   3   2   1

TABLE OF CONTENTS

ACKNOWLEDGMENTS

This manual was very much a product of a co-creative community. Sheila Krystal and Don Carlson provided the context and inspiration needed to initiate this project. My support network in Interhelp and Psychotherapists for Social Responsibility (ΨSR) helped me sustain my effort. My editorial consultant, Rosa Lane, is owed special thanks. Her facilitation and encouragement enabled me to complete the manual.

I particularly want to thank my sister, Nora Frenkel, an artist and teacher, for contributing the artwork for this book.

DEDICATION

This peace project is lovingly dedicated to Elissa Melamed. Elissa's courage, grace, and vitality inspired so many of us to take up the task of creating a peaceful world. Her loss is irreplaceable; her contributions invaluable.

"I don't know how long we have. We have to do this work because we believe in peace and in building peace. We start with ourselves, our communities: the circles get larger. If the bomb falls tomorrow, there's something so valid about living this way, that we would live this way anyway."

> — Elissa,
> talking at a Speakers' Training Workshop for
> Women's Action for Nuclear Disarmament
> Eugene, Oregon
> November, 1984.

SECTION I: Introduction—
A Personal Note

My earliest memories reflect war. Paris, 1940. German bombers skim over rooftops, their roars reverberate through the streets. A German soldier, green field cap and black boots, stoops down to offer me a cookie. My mother, tight-lipped, refuses the offer. The train station: giant locomotives spewing steam, groups of Wehrmacht officers and men mill about. Sounds echo under the glass and iron vaulted ceilings. We wait for the train to take us south to Spain, then to Lisbon. Our ultimate destination, New York Harbor.

Dreams and memories mingle. Before my birth my mother had a dream. She was in a train station, waving good-bye to me. I was on a troop-train, bound for the front. The dream frightened her for years.

I was born in Paris, August 1936. My parents are both Eastern European Jews. My mother grew up in Byelorussia, my father in southwest Poland. The Russian Revolution, the break-up of the Austro-Hungarian Empire, and the subsequent rise of Polish nationalism all contributed to their leaving their native lands and being in Paris in 1936. In August of that year, Madrid was being bombed by the fascists, the Berlin Olympics were in full swing, and three years remained before Europe would be swept into the devastation of WWII.

In October 1940, our ship sailed into New York Harbor. The Statue of Liberty elicited smiles and pleasure from all of us standing on the deck, eager for our first look at sanctuary. My father enjoyed teaching me my first words of English, right then and there: "How do you do?"

My adult life has been free of war's ravages. I was just a little too young for the Korean War, and a draft-exempt Yale graduate student in the field of psychology at the time of Vietnam. But my infancy and my roots in Europe where my father's parents and his sisters perished in the Holocaust, have sensitized me to issues of peace, war, and social justice throughout my life.

One of the first novels I read while still a pre-teen was *Black Boy* by Richard Wright. It vividly revealed to me the pain and humiliation caused by racial prejudice. My involvement in a socialist-zionist youth movement during my teen years broadened my perspective further. I saw how throughout history, people have exploited and oppressed each other. I also saw how in each generation, from Spartacus to King, people have been willing to take great risks in order to change social conditions.

My doctoral thesis explored the relation between racial prejudice and personality factors. After receiving my doctorate in 1964, I served as a consultant to a Headstart program in Harlem for three years. Since 1964, I have been a practicing psychotherapist. One of my most important teachers was Fritz Perls, the founder of Gestalt Therapy. I worked with him intensively from 1967 until his death in March 1970. During the late sixties and the seventies, I led gestalt trainings and workshops throughout the United States. As a gestalt leader at that time, I was part of a monumental shift in national consciousness. Perlsian Gestalt stressed the power of the individual to make choices counter to societal norms and expectations. It had a strong anarchistic, freedom-loving flavor which was congruent with other movements at that time such as the liberation of women and gays, black power, and the sexual revolution. All these trends, including Gestalt, shared a desire to change norms and the structures which constricted individual choice. By 1977, I felt that the Gestalt pendulum had swung too far in the direction of individualism, and had become part of what Christopher Lasch had dubbed "the culture of narcissism," in his book of that title. At that point I developed my ideas of a more balanced Gestalt approach which I expressed in my pamphlet: "Social Gestalt: A Response to Illusions of Freedom and Powerlessness." I also took part in the Gestalt Community Action Project, a group of Gestalt therapists who actively sought to develop a "Social Gestalt" therapy. We did this in conjunction with therapists who were part of the Third World community in the San Fran-

.cisco area. A number of my colleagues from G.C.A.P. are now active in the psychotherapeutic branch of the peace movement. I date the first flowering of this branch of the peace tree back to the spring of 1982.

Moving Into Peace Activism

My commitment to peace activism began then. A call was sent out to psychotherapists in the San Francisco Bay Area to come to a one day workshop focussing on our feelings about the nuclear threat to the planet. From that workshop grew an organization, Psychotherapists for Social Responsibility (ΨSR), which in spring 1985 had more than a hundred members. This organization and the Interhelp network* have served as an indispensable catalyst and support for my participation in the international awakening towards peace.

From the outset, I saw my role and the role of ΨSR as making explicit the connection between the personal and the political. In the summer of 1983, I experienced the interweaving of my personal destiny with my political work while leading a peace workshop for psychotherapists outside of Hamburg, Germany. I had been invited to Germany to do this workshop by a friend who had moved to Hamburg, and who wished to activate a network of peace therapists in that area.

I began the workshop by asking all of us to name the year in which we were born, and what our and the world's reality was at that time. I told the participants that I had been born in Paris, 1936, a time of Hitler's ascendency, and had been forced to flee France in order to survive. I let them know that many of my father's family in Poland had perished in Auschwitz, not far from the Galician town where they had lived. As we went around the circle each person told their story, many of those stories full of the pain and loss of war. I began noticing the agitation of the dark-haired woman sitting to my right. I had been the first to speak, and she was to be the last. When she

---

*See Resource Section

spoke, the room quickly stilled. She announced that she felt she had been born with poison in her veins. Her father was an S.S. man specializing in racial murder. Her early years were spent living in Nazi-occupied Galicia in an apartment taken from a Jewish family who had been exterminated.

Hearing her revelations, I felt the blood drain from my face, and thought, "My God, her father may have killed one of my relatives." Irony within ironies, something about the way her black, curly hair was set, and her whole appearance had reminded me of photos of my prewar Polish relatives. When she had finished, no one spoke. At that moment our mutual destinies had intersected, leaving us all moved and appalled. We knew the nature of the task that faced us. Old, deep wounds needed to be healed.

Monica, as I will call her, was driven by a blood-guilt. Blood of her murderer-father, blood of his victims. She carried the guilt that he had always dismissed.

During the workshop, her drivenness and self-hate lessened dramatically. I do not know the exact role I played in that transformation; but I do know that the feeling-tone of the workshop was one of compassion and self-acceptance. In the exercises, discussions, and individual work I did with participants, I stressed the importance of accepting and experiencing our thoughts and feelings, rather than condemning and rejecting them. Our appreciation of the preciousness of life and the universality of suffering also drew us closer together. At the workshop's close, Monica and I embraced each other fiercely. Our body contact did more than assure each other of our mutual support and acceptance. It sent a message to God and humanity, that love can triumph over bigotry and death. Less than a year after that workshop, I began creating this manual.

My Values and Building Peace

Certain values are of great importance to me. *They include full and free development of my human potential as I participate in and influence the world around me.* From these values stem my support for all those systematically denied their humanity because of sexism, racism, ageism and classism. I know that both the dispenser and recipient of these *isms* are diminished. We develop in relation to others' growth; we constrict when others constrict.

My emphasis with my clients is on helping them recognize their own process. When we see how we collude with internal and external blocks to full development, we can begin to work through those hindrances. From a sense of increased power in our own lives, we may then consider influencing our social environment.

It is from values such as these, that I have been moved to become active in the peace movement. Everyone's human potential is now endangered because of the nuclear threat. As a therapist and citizen involved in helping others develop their potential, my decision to become active in sustaining human life is both natural and imperative.

SECTION II: The Manual—
Uses & Principles

Uses

In its most general sense, the Peace Manual is one of count-less peace projects unfolding throughout the world. It is designed to increase our chances of evolving rather than extinguishing in the coming years. The text and exercises encourage you to explore the forces within and without you that bear on your participation in creating peace.

The manual may be used individually or within a group setting. When undertaken sequentially, it involves you in an ongoing process. After becoming acquainted with the use of visualization as part of completing this manual, you will move through sections on integrating the personal and the political; attitude change; empowerment; and spiritual aspects of peace work. The process then culminates in your creating a unique peace project. It is also possible to dip in and out of the manual. Each section stands on its own merits.

The Peace Manual may be useful for anyone interested in experiencing the interweavings between the personal and the larger social context, and for all who wish to build peace.

Principles

1. Definitions

Process—Working with Fritz Perls had a profound impact on the conduct of my life and work. It was from Fritz that I began to appreciate what I refer to in this manual as "process." We will return in depth to this concept later on; but first, here is our initial definition:

> Process is the ongoing *how* of existence.
> It stands in contrast to the *what* of existence.
> I am writing a book.
> *How* I write is my process.
> *What* I write is my product.

This seeming digression about process and product is vitally related to linking the personal and political. *How* we work toward peace (our process) is certain to effect the *what* of the world we help create (our product). That *how* is inextricably linked to our personal conditioning, values, and attitudes.

Whole-Brain Thinking—Most books rely heavily on the reader's left-brain functioning. That is, they deal with linear language and logic. Concepts are abstracted and evaluated; plots and information tracked and digested. These are all important left-brain activities. However, our right-brain provides us with the images, pictures, and wholistic "takes" which complement the linearity and conceptualizing of our left-brain functioning. Poetry is a good example of writing that is replete with invitations to right-brain activity.

I have included much right-brain imagery work in this manual in order to make the process of completing this manual an integrated, balanced one. You will have an opportunity to use both parts of your brain in each section of this book. Sometimes a guided fantasy or image will be suggested to you. Feel free to experiment with these suggestions and to substitute your own along the way.

This manual also invites your involvement and participation in completing it. Blank pages are part of the manual, to be filled at your discretion. By using your right-brain, and by helping to create this manual, you are reflecting in a microcosm another way of being, both politically and personally. Put in another way, full use of one's mental faculties and the sense of empowerment that comes through participating in an activity, are means toward attaining personal and political health.

2. Congruence Between Process and Content

I used imagery to help create this manual. My images included a wheel, a flag, and a spiral/helix. The spiral/helix was of particular interest to me since it corresponded to the nature of the manual's structure. That is, the manual is divided into sections; each section deals with similar issues on a different level at each stage. The vertical plane remains the same (the personal/political link), while different issues within that plane are developed. The final part of the spiral consists of constructing your own peace project.

I was further intrigued by the image of a helix corresponding to that of the manual when I realized that the biological building block of life, the DNA molecule, is also a helix. At first I tried to explain this coincidence logically, linearly. I soon discovered that I was trying to fit a non-linear image into a logical, linear frame to no avail. I dropped that attempt, and then simply developed my associations to this linking. Congruence between process and content emerged as a metaprocess, common to both the manual and biological life.

The manual's content has to do with the importance of process, utilizing our full potential, and empowerment in creating peace.

The process of completing this manual is congruent with the content. You are encouraged to develop your full potential through right and left brain exercises, and you help to create the manual itself. This process is congruent with a concept of peace which includes wholeness, and empowerment. This congruence between process and content is akin to that between function (process) and structure (content) in evolving biological life. We can call that congruence: integrity. A full correspondence exists between the function (process) and structure (content) of biological organisms. Evolution is in part a refining of this congruence. For instance the structure of a gill is perfectly suited to the function of drawing oxygen from water. This integrity can be seen as being present in all aspects of life.

Thus, both this manual and biological life share this inner congruence. The spiral/helix appears to be a universal structure reflecting/symbolizing this kind of integrity.

3. Process as a Motivator

Spirals, congruence, and such take me back to my reasons for writing this manual. Writing it would enable me to share my vision of the integral link between the personal and political; it would be a project of major dimensions for me, demanding time and effort on a scale comparable to my doctoral dissertation completed 20 years before. I had my doubts concerning my ability to carry out this project. Putting in all those hours with the hope that sometime in the future the manual might positively impact the peace movement was not enough incentive. Fame and fortune were even less of an incentive. Kudos from friends and family—nice, but still not enough.

It was only during the process of thinking and imaging about writing this book, that the clinching motivation emerged. During that process I discovered that my focusing on the link between the personal and political was helping me not only to see the link where I hadn't previously, it was also facilitating my development in building inner and outer peace. Thus I realized that the process of writing the manual could serve as a continuing source of learning and excitement. For a while I considered simply keeping a journal, a private source of discoveries, which I wouldn't have to edit or publish.

4. Making the Product Congruent with the Goal

I realized that a private journal was not a product congruent with the topic of linking the political and the personal. A journal is a private statement; a peace manual: an interpersonal, social, political one.

Deciding to go ahead and write a publishable manual then became the natural thing to do. That decision contributed greatly to my feelings of empowerment. Hopefully, working with this manual will encourage your own feelings of empowerment since it often brings you back to your inner resources.

From the richness of your own imagery work and concepts may spring a peace project. Each such project helps create peace in its own unique way. Working in concert and as individuals, we empower ourselves and each other in building a peaceful path.

SECTION III: The Manual—Our Initial Participation

Your participation in the manual begins here. We will begin with visualization, an invaluable vehicle for tapping our whole-brain thinking. Later in this section, you will have an opportunity to practice visualization as you explore personal images and ideas of peace.

1. Instructions for Visualizations

The Context—The use of mental imagery (visualizations) in problem solving, creative endeavors, personal development, and promoting physical well-being is becoming increasingly widespread. Underlying this trend is the assumption that part of our unconscious mind, whether it be called the "deep self" (Milton Erickson), the "higher self" (Assagioli), or the collective "unconscious" (Jung), can be a source of inspiration, wisdom and healing for us. Most of us do not know of the existence of this treasure. Indeed, many believe the contrary. Some of us are convinced that if we were to enter the cave of our unconscious, we would find only fearsome, loathsome creatures rather than a clear spring of inspiration. Thus, the existence and location of the treasure chest has been forgotten, the keys to open it misplaced. By beginning to believe that there is a place of wisdom, healing, and inspiration within all of us, we take an important first step on the path to internal and external peace. How then can we reach this valuable inner source?

Psychosynthesis, hypnotherapy and a variety of other psychotherapeutic disciplines describe the process which leads to tapping into that source.

The Process—The process involves a combination of relaxing and focusing. Relaxation is the first step, and can be furthered by slow, deep breathing. External stimuli are kept to a minimum. Distracting sights and sounds are kept in abeyance. It is wise to close one's eyes. The relaxation continues. You may wish to make a relaxation tape for yourself, which simply reminds you to pay attention to your breathing, and encourages you to breathe a little more deeply, a little more slowly. As you inhale, you take in breath deeply; as you exhale, let go. Occasionally, bring attention to other parts of your body: how your hands feel, how you feel in contact with the chair or bed in which you are relaxing. Thoughts may continue to skitter across your mind as you relax. Do not attempt to stop them; and, you needn't go along with them. Just notice them going by like leaves floating down a stream, or smoke rising from a chimney.

This process of relaxation is the first step toward contacting your source. Once you are in a relaxed state, use the following instructions from your left-brain to set the stage for your unconscious to send you the needed imagery.

(1) Imagine a setting in which you would like to meet the visualization. It could be a room, outdoors, on a raft, whatever.

(2) Give your unconscious a suggestion that it may be ready, at this point, to send you a visual image, symbol, or metaphor related to the topic you are exploring.

(3) When that image emerges, give it time to let it take on a life of its own. Allow it to be there without your trying to "figure it out" or "have it make sense." You may learn some interesting information from it if you engage this image in a dialogue. Speak to it; ask it questions. A further intensification and deepening of knowledge can come about when you switch places with the image and become it.

(4) When the dialogue has come to what appears to be a natural end, then return to an awareness of your breathing. Stay with your relaxed state for a while, and then open your eyes and come back in contact with your immediate surroundings, feeling awake and refreshed.

(5) Left-brain associations and interpretations are then

welcome. You needn't push or pull for them. They will emerge as needed.

There will be a number of instances while completing this manual, that you may wish to refer back to these instructions. You will have the opportunity to visualize as a way of discovering your blocks to empowerment, developing images of peace, and creating a peace project. Visualization can be an important aid in the process of building inner and outer peace.

2. A Note of Encouragement

For fifteen years I have helped workshop participants and psychotherapy clients utilize visualization as an adjunct to personal growth. I have noted that some people have more trouble visualizing than others. One source of difficulty lies in faulty expectations. Some of us expect our images to be clear and life-like, and dismiss vague, faint images as "not counting." Anything you see in your mind's eye may be treated as an important and valid source of information. It's also true that some of us differ in the ways in which we access information. Although most of us may primarily access visually, many use other sensory modalities. Thus, when asked to image peace, our response may be: a view of a serene landscape, the sound of wind chimes, the smell of bread baking, or the bodily sensation of relaxing. Whatever the nature of the image, welcome it as a source of guidance and information.

Visualizations, sensorial or pictorial, open up avenues of exploration, and often guide us into realms alive with fresh ideas and understandings.

They invite us into a world of possibility and abundance. We learn to tap into this world on its own terms, within its expansive context. This world of internal knowledge, once we learn to use it, provides an endless resource for growth, renewal, and guidance.

Let's begin our initial participation in the manual. We will begin with Exercise 1: An Image of Peace, our first visualization.

EXERCISE 1: An Image of Peace

Each one of us has our own unique image of peace. Let's start to visualize it right now. After closing your eyes and relaxing, instruct your unconsciousness to allow an image of peace to emerge for you. Welcome anything that comes before you. Your image of peace may be a past moment or moment yet to come. It may be a picture, a sensation, or even a feeling. This image may stand you in good stead in a variety of situations. It may be used as a guide to help you achieve a more peaceful internal state, as well as a reminder of a peaceful path when in a conflictual situation. Weaving peaceful images into our daily lives is one way of building internal peace. Find a way to record your image through drawing, writing, or another means comfortable for you.

When I did this exercise I came up with a memory of peace. The memory is that of a favorite beach of mine on the Russian River, north of San Francisco. There, people of different ages, classes, racial, and ethnic backgrounds all enjoy sunning, swimming, and picnicking. The idea is that of harmony. Different notes combine to create a pleasing sound: diversity within an interdependent whole.

Conflicts and Building Peace

However, we know that often differences and diversity lead to conflict rather than harmony. The broadbased, democratic peace movement is no exception. Peace workers are bound to hold differing views on both tactics and strategy. Conflicts arise and power plays are enacted. As a member of several peace organizations, I have witnessed and played a part in these storms. These struggles have been painful. Different individuals become attached to one approach or another; feelings of frustration and anger emerge. The political becomes very personal at such times. Often the tendency is to mask personal feelings of fear and anger by digging into a political position and righteously defending it. Abstractions and high-flown ideals fly around the room like rocks, while painful feelings grow in intensity. It is at these times that the peace worker is tested and tempered. Can s/he remain a peaceful worker? If we are working towards peace, how then do we deal with conflict between us in a peaceful manner?

EXERCISE 2: Thinking Peace

A number of questions emerge when we focus on the paradox of peace workers fighting. Some that I can think of are: What are some ideas and images I have about peace? How do I relate to conflict? Is my way of relating to conflict congruent with my image of peace?

I suggest that you consider these questions at this time, and allow yourself to see where your thoughts, images, memories take you when you do so. Give yourself all the time you need. You might wish to go back to deep breathing, so as to relax, thus allowing the relevant associations to move up more easily into your conscious mind.

A blank page is left for you here in order to note your answers to the questions.

When I answered these questions, my peace memory as well as ideas regarding conflict emerged. My memory of peace is the beach on the Russian River as I described above. I mentioned diversity as playing an important role in my peaceful image, different notes combining to create harmony, etc. Sometimes, however, differences lead to conflict. At those times I may try to avoid conflict, rather than face it. I realize that this does not work since my dissatisfaction still remains. My unexpressed dissatisfaction leads to deeper resentment and estrangement. I have learned that it is often better to overtly state my resentments and underlying wants if I am to feel an integral part of my surroundings.

I can recall times on the Russian River when loud radio playing or overzealous ball games interrupted my peaceful mood. I discovered that by peacefully letting the others know my wants, a mutual accommodation was reached. I have yet to encounter a belligerent response to my request. If and when I do, I hope I'll be able to meet hostility with peacefulness and firmness, rather than escalating the hostility.

In a sense, my peace process starts within me. I accept my wants, resentments, dissatisfactions, instead of trying to suppress them. I then can put them out into the world in a wholehearted manner. The peace process is thus initiated by my listening to myself, and affirming my ideas and feelings. The next step is to listen to the other, to listen with curiosity and compassion, to discover the other's point of view. How simple to state; how difficult to achieve. Certainly if we begin to compassionately and curiously listen to each other on an interpersonal, intergroup, and international level, we will be on the road to peace.

EXERCISE 3: Reflecting on Your Experience

Pause again, and reflect how you step on and off the peaceful path in your daily activities with your family, friends, coworkers, and neighbors. Choose a situation. How do you deal with conflict in this situation? You may wish to make some notes below.

Now that we have increased our awareness of some of our ideas, images, and experiences connected with peace, we may be ready to move on to the next portion of the spiral. The following section of this manual will enable us to explore specifically and deeply the ways in which we contribute to our state of inner peace or war.

SECTION IV: Integrating the Personal and Political

Ultimately we have just one moral duty:
to reclaim large areas of peace in ourselves,
more and more peace
and to reflect it towards others.
And the more peace there is, the more peace
there will also be in our troubled world.

—Etty Hillesum, *An Interrupted Life**

The Need for Integrating the Personal and Political

In June of 1983, as previously mentioned, I travelled to Germany to do peace and empowerment workshops at the invitation of friends in Hamburg and Wurzburg. One of the first questions I asked these groups was "What would you like to gain from this workshop?" I will paraphrase their invariable answer: "I want to be able to link the personal and the political in my life, and I have not seen a way of doing that. My hope is that this workshop will show me a path of integration."

These people's either-or experience with politics and the personal is universal. All too often, the personal and political have polarized, rather than complemented each other. Psychotherapists, by and large (although this is beginning to change), have been content to explore intrapsychic space with their clients without paying much attention to the forces of sexism, racism, and ageism, which affect all of us, and few consider the psycho-

---

* Pantheon Books, N.Y. 1983, p. 185

logical effects of the nuclear threat. On the other hand, political activists have jumped into the struggle without awareness of their process while doing their work. This has resulted in burnout, and bitterness among many activists who attempt to change the world without including themselves in the change. Aware individuals are thus faced with unbalanced models: health professionals who are unwilling to support or understand their political work; and political groups who don't understand the need for personal work and development.

Change needs to come in both directions. Psychotherapists, Psychologists, and Educators for Social Responsibility are organizations of health professionals encouraging their members to pay attention to the role that socio/political activism and empowerment can play in our healthy individuation and development.

Interhelp and other peace activists' organizations are realizing that it is important to pay attention to the mental and emotional health and development of their members if they wish the organization to flourish.

Peace Begins Personally

Whether the individual pursues personal growth, becomes an activist, or does both, we are still left with the individual initiating the process of building peace. We are the starting point. If we agree with the assumption that peace needs peaceful people in order to manifest, then we must answer the question: how do we help make ourselves more peaceful.

I believe that the road to internal peace is a long one. It is a process like any other, not something to be achieved in a few months time, or by reading one book or another. In my work as a therapist and therapee for the past 20 years, I have gathered tactics and theory in regards to creating inner peace which have been helpful to myself and my clients. I return to the image of the hidden treasure within us all.

Once I had a wonderful dream, in which I lived in a palace. A great, crystal chandelier sparkled high above me. What pleasure and joy I received taking in its light! That joy and peace which emerge for us in dreams and at times while near natural splendor are an indication of our inner potential.

Blocks to Internal Peace:
Self-criticality and Condemnation

Why, then, are we not at peace if that treasure shines deep within us all? One reason is the universal presence of self-criticism and condemnation. We are at war with ourselves. The critic is there as part of our socialization process. We have internalized the external critic in order to avoid punishment from the outside. We are constantly beating the world to the punch by striking ourselves. We never seem to be enough—smart enough, sexy enough, thin enough, rich enough, tough enough. Enough already! This criticism applies not just to our appearance and our behavior. It goes deeper than that. Our very emotions are suspect. We shouldn't be sad, angry, confused, open, tender, disappointed, up-tight, afraid. You name any emotion, and you'll probably find a time when you told yourself not to feel it. Thus the internal war rages on.

Frequently, a client comes to see me expecting me to act as an ally of the critic. The client wishes me to join forces with his/her critic in helping to root out and destroy the "subversive" thoughts and emotions that disturb him/her. I am seen as a psychologist, and as such, I am expected to have a diagnostic label that they then can pin on themselves. In any case, I am expected to ferret out their loathsomeness so that they can eventually emerge whole and healthy from our mutual endeavor.

When I refuse to play the role of ruthless ally, or of interventionist "big daddy," I am apt to encounter anger and indignation on the part of the client. If the client is willing to continue in psychotherapy long enough, s/he begins to learn that the "cure" comes about through self-acceptance and compassion, not from a continuation of self-hate and condemnation.

Fear as a Block to Internal Peace

Let us take our analysis of the causes of internal disquiet another step. I have mentioned that we often beat the world to the punch by criticizing ourselves. We can thus see that it is fear that underlies much of our harsh self-criticality. We are harsh to ourselves because we fear the judgement of others and/or because we have adopted the judgement of others since we fear their disapproval. Fear motivates our self-judgements without our knowing that it is present. Fear is the hidden controller, protected from detection by another fear: our fear of acknowledging our fear. We are afraid to admit our fears, and thus our fears continue to control us without interruption. I believe this dynamic is even stronger among men, who are conditioned to be fearless. If you are a man, to admit you're scared means you're a wimp or worse. After a while men succeed in pushing fear out of their consciousness, down into a hidden place where it thrives undisturbed.

Facing Our Fears and Self-criticality

Fear must be brought into the light—acknowledged, met, talked to—if we are to let go of our self-condemnations. To begin to look at our fears and our self-condemnation is a difficult and necessary task. Fears and self-condemnations are the rocks piled in front of the cave that holds the treasure of internal peace. Fears and self-condemnations must be recognized and gradually removed, stone by stone, from the cave's mouth. This task, itself, needs to be carried out in a spirit of compassion and acceptance. If we begin to look upon our fears and self-criticality with loathing then we are back to square one. It is here that the miracle of the treasure chest becomes apparent. Although it is usually sealed off from us, it can become available under certain circumstances. Thus, if we need to contact compassion and self-acceptance in order to do the work of facing our fears and criticality, we can use visualizations to help us make that contact.

EXERCISE 4: Contacting Your Compassionate Self

Take a few moments to check in with yourself at this time. See if it feels right to carry out a guided imagery exercise. If so, then begin the relaxation procedures outlined on page 14. Instruct your unconscious to send a visual image, symbol, or metaphor that can serve you as a compassionate guide. Having this guide as an internal resource will serve you well when you face some of your fears and self-judgements as part of your work in completing this manual. The compassionate part of ourselves often needs to be developed. It is a unique blending of our head and heart, combining, as it does, both understanding and love. Most of us sorely need our own compassion. That compassion can be a bridge of peace, connecting us to ourselves and others. Find a way to document your image, symbol or metaphor through drawing, painting, collage or writing. This poem contains my image of compassion.

Compassion

We each can our own jailor be,
or give a rose to make us free.
A rose that glows eternally,
a rose that's named compassion.
And when we turn to share this rose
then others shed their heavy loads
to sweetly savor their repose
and feel their own compassion.

Use the space below to document your image.

Our Experience with Psychological Violence

I once heard a group leader say that, in a way, we are all mass murderers. We have all ruthlessly wiped out hundreds of feelings within ourselves, and tried to do the same with others. Before we can build peace at home and in the world, we need to acknowledge both our capacity for violence, and how we have all suffered as a result of violence. By violence in this case, I mean psychologically wiping out, invalidating a person's existence. All of us have had the experience of:

(a) being wiped out
(b) wiping ourselves out
(c) wiping someone else out.

EXERCISE 5: Remembering Wipe-outs

I suggest you do the following exercise to experience, more fully, the role that psychic violence has played in your life. By immersing yourself in the shadow you can better appreciate and strive for the light. I have purposely preceded this particular exercise with one in which you had the opportunity to contact a compassionate part of yourself. Any time you need to contact that part while doing the next exercise, feel free to do so. Breathe deeply. Place your hand on that part of your body where the compassionate part resides. Allow your compassionate self to be present.

In this exercise, remember that you can go as deeply as you choose, and return to the here and now whenever you wish. Begin by attaining a state of deep relaxation. Next, imagine yourself in a long passageway with three doors. Behind each door is a memory of a time when either you were wiped out, you wiped yourself out, or you wiped somebody else out. The exercise consists of spending some time, as much as feels right, behind each of those doors. Remember you can call on your compassionate self to be there for you if and when you need it.

When you have finished being behind all three doors, spend some time with your compassionate self. Then go back behind these doors again, but this time with a more positive sense of yourself. Play the scenes again, but meet the wipe-out in a different way. Return to the here and now, feeling renewed and refreshed.

Review the above instructions carefully, and then do the exercise.

As we become sensitized to our tendencies to violate ourselves, to violate others and to collude with others in our own violation, we become less likely to engage in that kind of behavior. Internal fear, self-criticality, and psychological violence all contribute to an atmosphere conducive to war. When we fear, and wish to wipe out our own tendencies, thoughts, and feelings—then we are likely to endow others with these "shadow" parts of ourselves. We project the forbidden parts of ourselves onto others. We then attack the other for harboring those properties which we detest in ourselves. We seek out and find enemies, whether they are close to us, or in the form of whole nations or races. Thus fear and self-hate fuel the psychological fires that lead to war.

Creating Internal Peace

There's more than one way to skin a cat (what a barbarous expression, let's follow its dictates and say instead, there's more than one way to make a bouquet). Creating peace within needn't hinge solely on recognizing and confronting our tendencies towards self-criticality, fear, and violence. Other complementary tactics may also be useful. These include (1) relaxation, (2) meditation, (3) affirmation, and (4) visualization. All these approaches can serve to promote a sense of peace, harmony, and well-being when they are incorporated into the texture of your life. These approaches to self-healing and self-development are alike in that they require time/space away from the daily hurly-burly. Sometimes that might be only a matter of seconds or minutes, but even then, a shift in focus from the external to the internal is required.

The Rhythm of Contact/Withdrawal

In order to make that shift with awareness and self-support, the process of contact/withdrawal needs to be understood. Rhythms and cycles are part of the natural world. The tides flow in and out; the fields yield abundance and then lie fallow before becoming fertile again; our heart pumps blood out and in; our breath takes air out and in. The lion energetically stalks, chases, and devours its prey, and then spends hours lazily basking in the sun. Nature has its rhythm; we humans seem to forget ours. We try to fit ourselves into the rhythm of machines, organizations, and bureaucracies. We forget the natural rhythms both outside and inside ourselves. We fly into other time zones and confuse our inner clocks further. Out of balance, we turn to stimulants and soporifics to achieve a balance we have lost long ago. By remembering contact and withdrawal, we recall our need to follow our natural rhythms. There are times when we need to be in contact with the external world—with the people, tasks, and problems we are facing. Equally crucial, and all too often we forget our natural need for withdrawal. Our need for time to be with ourselves, to regain our energy, to be refreshed and healed by that inner source we all possess. Our society is a "doers" society, not a contemplative one. The pressure coming at us from all sides is to constantly be out there, performing, competing. We lose our balance when we continually comply with those demands.

Wiping ourselves out with excessive t.v., alcohol, or drugs is not a satisfactory way to redress the balance. What is needed is the ability and will to go back inside to the healing sources within. Tapping these sources leads to true refreshment and balance. Withdrawal need not mean an hour's meditation each day. It can be incorporated into the ongoing rhythm of your day. For example, my clients know, since I talk to them about contact and withdrawal, that I do not give them my undivided attention for all of the time we spend together. There are times, sometimes just 10 or 15 seconds, when I look out my office window and enjoy watching the birds and plants in my garden. Other times when I get in touch with my breathing, my feet on the floor. By paying attention to my process of contact/withdrawal, I'm able to carry out a full day of work without feeling drained.

Four Approaches to Creating Inner Peace

For anyone who wishes to become more politically active, in addition to continuing to raise a family and/or earn a living, it's advisable to learn/utilize any one or more of the four approaches listed below.

(1) *Relaxation.* There are many ways of achieving a relaxed state. Autogenic Training, bio-feedback, and auto-hypnosis are

some of the most popular. You don't have to make a big deal of this (or any of the approaches). Relax! If you smiled just now that's good—humor is a great relaxant; but where can you find funny relaxation therapists? Remember, slow deep breathing can't hurt as long as you don't have a spear stuck in your side.

(2) *Meditation.* If I begin to list all the different ways of meditating, it'll take up the rest of the manual. If I mention some, people will feel left out. In short, there are many types of meditation that you can learn. Some come with more spiritual ballast than others. You can meditate on a concept, an image, a point in space, your breathing, or whatever emerges into your awareness. Most meditation will quiet your brain wave activity, and serve to refresh you. Some meditation can help you to gain perspective and distance from the mundane grind. Meditation can affect your self-esteem either positively or negatively; positively because you can go around telling people that you meditate; negatively, if you suspect that you're not doing it right.

(3) *Affirmations.* Many people swear by these. Some swear at them. Affirmations are positive statements about yourself which you repeat at regular intervals on a daily basis. The most famous is Coue's "Every day in every way I am getting better and better." That one covers all the bases. If you want to be more specific, that's fine. Keep saying each day that you're a good person, and you might eventually believe it. My favorite affirmation is, "I'm so great I don't need affirmations."

(4) *Visualizations.* Describing the myriad positive uses of visualization would take up another book. As a matter of fact it's taken up at least ten. You have already done a number of visualizations as part of participating in this manual. They can be used to summon up positive parts of yourself, and help you with problem solving. In addition, they can aid you in finding which approaches are most helpful to you at this point in your life. Learn to experiment with visualizations; find out how to use them most effectively. Send me a stamped, self-addressed envelope with one dollar, and I will send you a guided fantasy that will help you discover the best times in the day for you to use any of these approaches. Better yet, visualize my receiving your request and my answer; that way you save a dollar and postage.

The Process of Our Lives

Humor, respect for our inner rhythms, self-regard and compassion, all play a role in developing our ability to live in inner peace and harmony. Any or all of the four approaches described above can also be helpful in that process. How we weave together these ingredients and more, each of us in our unique way, is what determines the process of our lives.

> "I must stop and listen to myself, sound my own
> depths, eat well and sleep properly if I am to
> keep my balance. . . . But alas, the emphasis these
> days is on speed, not on rest." *

These words of Etty Hillesum can be taken to heart by many of us. In the midst of the terror of the Nazi occupation of Holland, this young Jewish woman sought a way to maintain her clarity and balance so that she might better serve herself and others.

In the face of the nuclear threat, we are presently all hostages to terror. Instead of the yellow star that the Jews of Nazi-occupied Europe were forced to wear, perhaps we could choose to wear mushroom-cloud stick-ons. Thus, our awareness of imminent danger would be made more apparent to everyone.

Those of us who do not deny, who have acknowledged the universal danger, particularly need to pay attention to our process of living. We face the existential anxiety of living in a world that could be judged dangerously insane, were we to anthropomorphize it. I recall a client saying, "I'd rather think that I'm crazy, than believe that the whole world is." Alas, the situation is not either-or. We must deal with our internal violence and disquiet within a dangerously unbalanced world. Thus, clearing up our self-criticality and fears, promoting our own self-acceptance and compassion, healing ourselves and maintaining our balance through the use of visualizations, meditation, affirmations, and relaxation are processes we need to explore if we

---

* *An Interrupted Life*, p. 31

are to avoid despair and burn-out. The process, the very texture of our lives and how we live them, needs to reflect a concern with achieving inner harmony if we are to become effective peacemakers.

To achieve inner harmony requires a realistic connection with the outer reality constantly going on all around us. If we are not in balance with the outer, we cannot have inner harmony. Three relevant aspects of the greater picture are: process as duration, others as support, and acknowledging conflict.

Process as Duration

There is another meaning to the word process which bears examining. That is, process not as the how of an activity, but as a word describing an activity which extends over time and has different phases. Giving birth is a process. So is writing a book, building a house, or doing psychotherapy. Every process has a beginning, middle, and end.

How, then, does this meaning of process relate to creating peace? My first association is to impatience. Impatience seems endemic to our western civilization. Many recent technological advances have served to increase our expectations regarding quick, if not instant gratification of our desires. We use microwave ovens, communicate in a minute with others thousands of miles away, expect instant enlightenment from cassettes and books. We rarely bake our own bread, or even see a chicken except in plastic wrapped hunks in the supermarket. As our expectations for the "quick fix" rise, we become increasingly impatient when we are faced with natural processes which need to take their own time. Personal development and changes in political/social consciousness are both areas in which impatience can serve to disrupt an ongoing process of change. Pushing too hard, too fast, leads to backlash and can be counterproductive.

The process of building a world of peace will not be accomplished in one generation. War may be averted; but the world of non-war is not equivalent to a world of peace. Those of us who are involved in facilitating growth processes, such as farmers, teachers, psychotherapists, and artisans, realize the importance of time in relation to real change. That awareness must be carried over into building peace, lest we become discouraged and leave the task half-done. Half-done is worse than not done at all, since it is an indication of wasted effort, discouraging others from joining in the effort to build peace. The farmer doesn't stop weeding his fields in mid-May even though no edible vegetables have yet emerged. The work that we do plants seeds which may take generations to come to full fruition. If we accept the length of the process and believe that it is worth the wait, then we can go about our tasks with patience and confidence.

Once, while vacationing in Mexico, I walked on a beach, and saw a fisherman throwing his net into the water. Again and again he would throw the net in and pull it out. Sometimes he succeeded in gathering in the fish, other times not. In Spanish, I said, "You must have patience to be a fisherman." "Yes," he replied, surprising me with the rest of his response, "if you pull in the net too fast, the fish tend to get away."

EXERCISE 6: Process as Duration in Your Life

Think about your life, your goals, and development. Can you see the edges of a process that you have completed, are completing or are beginning? Think about the time spans. Remember the ones that have taken years.

You may use the blank space below to note your associations, memories, and thoughts about process as duration.

Acknowledging Conflict

As creators of peace we need not be conflict-phobic. Peace itself is not a static state. It is linked to the untrammelled expression of ideas. "Pax Romana" or "the peace of the graveyard" are not what we strive for. Change and development, conflict and synthesis are part of my vision of peace. What is important is how we deal with conflicts. If conflicts are repressed or suppressed they will emerge later in one unpleasant form or another. When we begin to listen to ourselves, and to listen to others, then the possibility of a dynamic peace arises. Fritz Perls stated, "contact is the appreciation of differences." This is a very difficult lesson to learn and practice. When we remember our conflicts with our friends, families, and love partners we immediately realize how difficult. Yet it can be a cornerstone attitude contributing to a consciousness that will help bring peace. Harmony and peace both involve allowing different notes to arise; they then interact in such a way as to create a new whole, transcending the sum of the parts.

Others as Support

To be able to face the insanity and destructiveness of our present world is a scary task indeed. To do it alone, without support, is asking too much for many of us. I know that with all the personal work that I have done on and for myself, I could not have written this book or carried out many of my peace activities without the support of my "affinity" group in ΨSR. For years we have met on a regular basis and given each other the time and space needed to deal with the conflicts, confusion, and despair that are part of our lives as peace activists. We also share joy, excitement, and well-being when some of us have successfully delivered a talk, held a workshop, or carried out a project. Our mutual sharing and support give us the heart to continue.

Dealing with building peace in a group setting seems altogether congruent and appropriate. Peace may initially emanate from within, and then be experienced and transmitted through groups of people sharing similar visions. Finding and/or creating such a group can be an important step for an individual walking the path of peace.

The Group as Support for the Individual

When we being thinking about politics and personal development, the issue of group vs. individual needs inevitably arises. One task of building peace is to heal that dichotomy. We need networks, organizations, and groups each having their own ways of working towards peace, and each honoring the creative impulses of their members. The group, rather than being seen as demanding a certain behavior from its members, becomes a context wherein each individual has an opportunity to develop his/her capacities more fully. My image of a peace group is that of a garden, from which a variety of plants can grow and flourish, rather than a top/down hierarchy molding members to carry out predetermined tasks.

In order for peace groups to resemble that model, members must make a conscious effort to be aware of process in the group.

How are meetings conducted? What is the feedback loop like? Is the system open to exchange and new input? Is humor encouraged? What about use of right-brain approaches in order to tap into more than just the cognitive parts of our experience? Do we listen to the heart as well as the right-brain/left-brain head? A congruent peace group or organization will ideally be an open system encouraging and eliciting the creativity of its members. Remember, watch the process and then hopefully feel empowered enough to do something about it when there's something that could use your attention.

EXERCISE 7: Visualizing and Expressing Your Peace Image

We all have our ideas about peace. Now you may wish to give yourself a chance to contact your personal image of peace. It may be the same one that you met before, or it may have changed. After relaxing sufficiently, call upon your unconscious to send up an image, visual metaphor or symbol, representational of peace. Stay with the image for awhile, breathing deeply; find a place in your body where you can keep that image. Then imagine the image right there, and breathe directly into it. When you think you can do this exercise with your eyes closed, then close your eyes, take some quiet, deep breaths, and begin.

Use the following blank space to make a visual representation of your image. Draw it, paint it, whatever. You needn't be shy, nobody's going to grade you for artistic ability except your own judge, and you can send him/her on vacation. This is an image you can come back to as part of meditation or visualization work in the weeks and months to come.

Recapping

The personal and political are different aspects of our inner and outer reality. When we are oppressing and fighting ourselves, we are more likely to contribute to war-making than creating peace. Psychological violence tends to spread, as does inner harmony. In the face of the nuclear peril, we need to pay special attention to the very texture of our lives if we are to effectively work towards promoting a dynamic peace.

Nora Frenkel

SECTION V: Attitude Change

Ambivalence to Change

For a stable, world-wide peace to be created, the attitudes of millions must undergo a change. Immediately, we are faced with our ambivalence to any kind of change. We want change and yet we resist change. An example is that of the person seeking out psychotherapy. S/he is in pain, s/he knows that something is wrong, and hopes that by seeing a therapist their pain will abate. S/he soon discovers that in order for the pain to abate attitudes and behavior will have to change. Ah, there's the rub. For to change, means to venture into the unknown. Many find it better to hang onto whatever scraps they have, moldy though they may be, than to let go of the familiar and reach out for something new. The ambivalent push-pull becomes apparent. The client wants to change and is afraid to do so.

In the larger sphere of working towards peace, we have a situation full of pain and danger. We know that something is wrong and must be tended to. But here again, the rub emerges. If we are to take part in the awakening towards peace, we will have to change some of our attitudes and behavior, to leave the familiar, and start a new journey.

Our ambivalent attitude towards change should not cause us alarm. I believe it is an inherent part of our humanness. Within each of us is a force that works toward stability and homeostasis on both a physiological and psychological level. It is a force we can see as helping us to survive. Within each of us there is another kind of force; one that pushes us towards transcendence and innovation. That force has helped us to evolve. Sometimes these forces work at cross purposes; sometimes they complement each other. What is different about this particular time in the history of the human race, is that we must innovate and transcend in order to survive as a race. The innovation must come in the area of learning to live peaceably with each other on all levels, including the international one.

EXERCISE 8: Meeting the Challenge

The need for meeting this planetary challenge may seem abstract and remote to you at present, and yet it is likely that you yourself have been faced with analogous situations in your own life. Give yourself a moment now to think of times in your life when you faced a major block or threat, a challenge which led you to take innovative action to insure your survival. Use the space below to note these examples.

Two Attitudes Central to Building Peace

There are two specific attitudes which must become prevalent if the work of building peace is to succeed. First, we need to recognize that there is an imminent danger to all humanity because of the presence of nuclear weapons on the planet. Second, we must acknowledge that each individual can help in building peace.

Denial of the Nuclear Threat

Currently, information alerting us to the nuclear threat is available. However, providing people with information as to the apocalyptic consequences of nuclear war doesn't always convince them that the chances of a nuclear holocaust occurring are very great, and that chances of surviving one are very small.

Both cognitive and emotional elements play a role in the acceptance of new information. If the information appears too threatening, and if there appears to be little we can do about the new state of affairs, our natural response is one of denial or blocking. An analogous situation is that of the medical patient who has just been informed that they have a terminal illness. Elizabeth Kubler-Ross and others have noted that the initial response is one of denial.

As the disease progresses and the patient becomes progressively incapacitated, it becomes more difficult for the patient to maintain their denial system. S/he may then move into the later stages which include anger, resignation, and finally, acceptance. In the case of denial of the threat of nuclear holocaust, there is no progressive debilitation. No series of "small" nuclear explosions. Massive death may come very swiftly, the life support system of the planet extinguished in a matter of hours. One day, the crowd's bustling, the cafe's crowded, the sun is shining on green grass and flowers; the next, fire and greyness everywhere, no crowds, no sun or green grass, only a universal pall. Thus the mechanism of denial is not threatened by external events. Only our imagining, based on sound scientific evidence, enables us to see the threat clearly. Many of us choose not to imagine, but to deny instead. However, denial becomes increasingly difficult to maintain in the face of wide public concern about the threat. Many peace and professional organizations are letting people know that there is a threat and that we had better face it.

EXERCISE 9: Your Nuclear Story

Look back, when did you first become aware of the scope and intensity of the danger? Where and how did you begin to deny that danger? What are the factors, events, people who have helped you to drop denial as a defense, and move on to considering action?

Give yourself some time to consider these questions. You may consider discussing the above questions with people whom you know. Find out their responses. They may still be in a denial mode. Listen to them, and find out more about the forces within us which keep us from facing unpleasant facts. Approach such a discussion without trying to change their attitudes. When you listen, they will be less defensive, more ready to admit their ambivalent feelings. Good listening on your part may yield greater knowledge.

Use the following space to write your answers to the above questions, or any other thoughts/images you may have about the issue of denial of the nuclear threat. Results of discussions with others can also be noted in the following space.

Denial of Our Power

Even when we stop denying the danger, there is still another attitude with which we must deal. This one holds that "nothing we do will make a difference anyhow." This underlying pessimistic/cynical assumption is tied into the denial of the fact of the threat. If we are convinced that we can do little to prevent world holocaust, why bother paying attention to it. Why not just become "Epicureans for Social Irresponsibility" and fiddle while it all burns.

The roots of these underlying pessimistic assumptions are tied into factors mentioned in the next section on empowerment. If we have a history of being unable to affect our surroundings, it is likely that we will be pessimistic about our chances for avoiding war. Some of us block ourselves from seeing what steps to take even if we did have the power to influence events. Each of us is then left with an attitude of, "I'm not going to take this stuff seriously, because even if I did, there's nothing I or others can do about it. Even if we could do something, I can't think of anything to do, anyhow. So it's best to try to forget the whole thing, and enjoy life as much as I can. Maybe it won't happen. So pass me a (a) beer, (b) quiche, (c) joint, and let's talk about (1) our hangups, (2) our work, (3) the weather, instead." If this simulated quotation sounds confused and self-defeating, that's only because it is both those things.

Notice that the attitude of powerlessness tends to be self-perpetuating. The person doesn't bother to think about possible solutions since s/he doesn't believe anyone will listen anyhow. S/he doesn't believe anyone will listen because s/he can't think of a solution. This chain of thought keeps the individual powerless, and more prone to acting out anger at being powerless through self-destructive addictions. Thus, not only are these attitudes harmful to the individual in question, they tend to remove that person from the ranks of those who believe it is possible to work for and attain peace. A pity, since I believe we need all the help we can get.

Facts vs. Beliefs

Although it is a fact that we are in great danger of extinguishing life on earth if a nuclear war takes place, we do not know for a fact that our collective efforts will prevent such a war. It is certainly in the realm of possibility that even if each one of you reading this book became a peace activist, a nuclear holocaust could still take place.

In this area we are operating on the basis of beliefs, not facts. I believe that our efforts can make a difference. That we will cause others to awaken, that the ripples will continue to grow, until the combined effect of all the ripples will cause a great wave of peace to put out the fire of war. That is my belief which sustains me in reaching out to a variety of groups whether they be German students, Esalen seminarians, business people, or psychotherapists. I believe that my acting in concert with others can contribute to building peace. I know that in choosing to work for peace I have enriched my life.

The Consequences of Belief

Facts are facts; we can either acknowledge or ignore them. Beliefs are different. We can choose them. I choose to believe that my activism helps build peace; someone else chooses to believe that activism is futile. Neither one of us knows for sure which belief adheres most closely to the truth, although we both may think we do. However, one thing is certain in the matter of beliefs. Your belief will affect your behavior. Thus, if we choose to believe that our efforts can make a difference, it is more likely that we will be more hopeful, zestful and engaged in life. If we believe that our efforts will be for naught, then it is more likely we will be less engaged, and more liable to take part in self-destructive activities.

When we take on the mantle of protectors of the planet and its people, our attachment and sensitivity to its beauty and richness grows. We begin to cherish our human race and planet and revel in it. Those who see no hope or purpose withdraw their energy from the people and planet, and become smaller as a result. These statements are more than beliefs; they are knowledge based on my own growth and the growth I have observed among my friends in the peace movement over the last several years.

Camus once said, "when a man reaches thirty-five, he is responsible for his face." Our beliefs shape our actions; our actions influence our beliefs. We create ourselves constantly in the image of those beliefs. My association at this moment involves some of the Roman statues that were part of the traveling Vatican Exhibit. The chiseled faces of the Roman legionnaires exuded a cold, almost insensate, ruthlessness; the faces of the persecuted saints radiated peace and gentleness.

EXERCISE 10: Self Beliefs

Now it is your chance to go within yourself and see what memories, ideas, and images emerge for you around the area of beliefs. These beliefs need not be connected to the issue of building peace. They may be beliefs you hold, which are related to your personal growth and development. For instance, do you believe that you can develop and change? That you are a positive addition to the universe? Give yourself a chance to relax, take all the time and space you need. When you are relaxed you can then begin to allow thoughts and images related to some of your basic beliefs about yourself to emerge. Stay with them for as long as it seems fruitful, and then come back to the manual. You may use the following blank page to make notes of your findings.

Saliency

Attitude change is not enough. In order for attitudes to be translated into action, another variable must be present. This is the factor called saliency. If an attitude is salient, that means that it is often in the foreground of consciousness. It is quite possible to read a book, see a movie, go to a workshop, and for that period of time and shortly thereafter, have the issue of the nuclear threat be salient for you. But what happens as the days and weeks go by? These attitudes of knowing the danger and believing that you can do something about the threat begin to fade. It's not that they are contradicted, just that they are no longer salient, and thus are less likely to contribute to behavioral change.

Keeping Attitudes Salient

There are, however, at least three different ways that we can keep an attitude or set of attitudes salient.

1. *Emotional Bonding*. The more connections we can establish between our attitude (which is cognitive in nature) and the emotional parts of ourselves, the more likely our attitude will remain salient.

Allow your feelings to be there when you discuss or think about this whole area. Sadness, rage, despair, love for the planet, are all emotions that are natural responses to the threat, and they serve as a booster to the attitudes. Sensory input of different kinds is also important. Songs, films, movement, art, all connected to loving our planet and ourselves, strengthen the saliency of these attitudes. Participating in any or all of these activities can be helpful. Singing one song, or writing one poem can be worth hearing a thousand words on the subject.

2. *Bolstering*. This is a term used by attitude change researchers, which refers to post-attitude behavior designed to reinforce the shift in attitudes that has taken place. An example of bolstering is the person who, after buying a car, then visits friends in order to get agreement that his/her choice was the

correct one. There are magazines, periodicals, and books available which can serve to bolster those of us wishing to keep our attitudes about building peace salient. There are also many organizations which provide personal contacts, and structured opportunities for involvement. I have listed relevant publications and organizations in the resource section at the back of the manual.

3. *Participation and Action.* Attitudes predispose us towards action. The reverse is also true. By taking action we strengthen the attitude which is congruent with the action taken. It is as if an unconscious part of ourselves is saying: "If I did that action, I must have had a good reason." We usually do not like to think of ourselves as acting without having a good reason, and a specific attitude can provide that reason. It is also likely that the more innovative the action, the stronger reinforcement the attitude receives. For instance, during the 40 days that the Fast for Life lasted in 1983, I experimented with new kinds of behavior. One of those actions involved me standing on the street and handing out leaflets. This was a difficult task I had assigned myself, since I find intruding into someone else's space abhorrent. Can you imagine a diffident, tactful leaflet-passer? Well, I tried. In any case, doing that challenging task certainly played a part in reinforcing and making salient my attitudes about the importance of peace work.

Compartmentalization

Another psychological phenomenon which has a bearing on attitudes/actions is compartmentalization. We compartmentalize on both a conscious and an unconscious level in order to increase our efficiency. Certain attitudes are relevant within certain contexts. In church you think about ethics; at the office, about making money.

In the area of peace activism, we can notice how compartmentalization serves to limit the scope of our outreach. A personal example. I was an active member of the Gestalt Institute of San Francisco for many years. Because of compartmentalization, I saw the Gestalt Institute strictly in terms of issues related to gestalt therapy. It was the staff itself that asked me to organize a meeting around the theme of the nuclear threat. I had not thought to offer such a meeting. Somehow my attitudes about the Institute were in one compartment, and my attitudes about the nuclear threat were in another.

This kind of compartmentalization has dissolved as I have become more engaged in linking the personal and political. I realize that we are all faced with the threat of planetary holocaust; and thus, every person or group of people are involved in this issue. My outreach has expanded as a result of this realization. College students, business people, neighbors, colleagues, Europeans, the Esalen community, are some of the diverse groups of people with whom I have met around this issue.

EXERCISE 11: Dissolving Compartments

Now give yourself a chance to think about the people and groups whom you would approach were you to "spread the word." You might include friends, family, associates, parent's groups, religious congregations, athletic teams, business clubs, to begin mentioning a few possibilities. Let networking sources pop up for you without critical feedback such as "Oh, they wouldn't be interested." You may come up with some surprising information. Use the following blank space to make notes.

EXERCISE 12: What Has Influenced
Your Attitudes?

Now, use the next blank page to draw some conclusions about your own attitude change. Where have you noticed a shifting of your attitudes in the area of peace-building, or any other socio-political topic? What influence helped that shift to occur? What part did personal contact play? The media? Publications? Did your participation in an event related to these topics such as a teach-in, rally, meeting, have an effect on your shift? What do you think are some of the most potent ways to influence people's attitudes on these issues?

SECTION VI: Empowerment

A Definition

The word "empowerment" has become part of the jargon in many political/psychological circles. Simply stated, empowerment means realizing that we have a greater ability to affect our environment than we thought we had. Environment may encompass life partner, family, workplace, and may extend to larger political structures.

This definition rests on the individual developing a new way of perceiving his or her relationship to the environment. Thus no one can empower another. We can only empower ourselves and/or encourage others to do the same. We all have to do our own thinking and our own empowering.

Disempowerment and Its Results

Our conditioning, especially if we are women or members of underprivileged minorities, encourages us to limit our perception of our own power. We are all born into a power structure: our family, where the power resides in the adults. For many years, we, as children, have generally been taught, both directly and indirectly, that we do not have much say about our environment. This is not good training for people who are then expected to become responsible, self-directed adults. Many of the institutions we attend as children, religious and educational, are also "top-down" hierarchies, where our feedback has little effect on what occurs. Fitting into the mold, whether at home, in the school or university, or at places of worship, is rewarded in a variety of ways. Contacting our needs and expressing them, when they contradict those held by the powerful, is punished. Compliance, defiance, and all the self-destructive ways of doing either, are the result of this system. Indirect ways of self-destructive compliance include compulsive achievement- and approval-oriented behavior. We sometimes lose touch with our deeper wants and needs in order to receive rewards from powerful others. Indirect, self-destructive defiance includes all the various addictions. Drugs, alcohol, sexual promiscuity can be seen as telling societal expectations to jump in the lake. Unfortunately, the expectations remain, and the defiant one is left floundering and drowning in that metaphorical lake.

EXERCISE 13: Recalling Disempowerment

You may wish at this point to imagine the bubbles rising from that lake. Close your eyes and let yourself take ten deep breaths.

Now that you are somewhat more relaxed, let yourself go back into that quiet place, and recall times in your life when you felt your power limited by others. Track your responses as you remember those times.

The following blank space is an opportunity for you to write down some of these incidents and your present response to them.

We Disempower Ourselves

While others have imposed limits on our wants and our sense of power and purpose, we also have within us, forces which gladly collude with such external impositions. If others make decisions for us, we can make them responsible when things go awry. We can also enjoy the fruits of their decisions without having had to make risky efforts in gaining them. Fear, sloth, inertia, all play a part in our colluding with those who would limit our power. Each of us has within ourselves a part that would just as soon "let George do it."

EXERCISE 14: Visualizing Your "Colluder"

In this exercise, I suggest that you first review the instructions regarding visualization found on page 14 of the manual. When you feel ready, find the comfortable place where you can begin the relaxation process. The deep breathing and subtle letting go that accompany this process can be savored. Eyes may be closed or partially open, whichever induces the most relaxation. When you are ready, you may suggest that your unconscious mind send you an image of that part of yourself which colludes in disempowering you. Use the space below to make notes, drawings, etc. pertaining to your image.

When I carried out this exercise, the following story/images emerged: I am in a room in an institution. I realize it is a visitors' room in a jail. I am visiting that part of myself which I call "the colluder." The colluder is a short, wiry man, who exudes fear and nervousness. He smokes, bites his nails and taps his feet while talking to me. He is angry at me because I frighten him. I realize that I could be in jail, and that he could be the visitor, if I don't watch out. As the colluder, my primary feelings are those of fear and irritation. As myself, I begin to think of the colluder as a fidgety, scared child. I take him out of the jail to an old pine tree overlooking the ocean. There I cradle him and comfort him. He becomes younger and younger. When he is a baby, I imagine being his mother and nursing him. I imagine being him and nursing. I take deep breaths while imagining. I come back to my room feeling relaxed and whole.

This image gave me some important clues as to the role fear plays in my giving away my power. I also realized that in addition to being frightened, I also have the power to nourish and comfort myself. Realizing that I have that power is part of my becoming empowered.

The Movement Towards Empowerment

Empowerment is catching. The civil rights movement, women's and gay liberation, the move towards sharing decision-making in the workplace, are all signs of a strong trend in the U.S. towards disempowered segments of our society acknowledging their power. I believe that grassroots peace work is the latest and most powerful wave reflecting this movement toward empowerment.

People of all ages and classes throughout this country are realizing that nuclear war is a distinct possibility, and that it would affect them directly and drastically. A nuclear winter, which might very well destroy the life-support system of this planet, would be the result of even a "limited" exchange of nuclear weapons. By each person making their voice for peace heard, and by helping others to do the same, our feelings of empowerment and the chance for peace grow.

Many of us do not want to give our power away in this area. The stakes are too high; the risks are too great. We are forced by the threat to acknowledge the extent to which we have given away our power. Millions in the U.S. and throughout the planet are beginning what Jonathan Schell calls "the awakening." It is not only an awakening to danger, it is also an awakening to the power we had not acknowledged was present—the power we have to create a world of peace.

EXERCISE 15: Four Steps to Facilitate Empowerment

1. Recall times in your life when you have been/felt empowered. What were the circumstances? What internal and external factors fostered those feelings; what factors inhibited them? Use the space below for notes.

2. Do a visualization. Ask to be shown that part of you that sees and encourages your empowerment. Engage in a dialogue with it. Discover some guidelines designed to increase your sense of empowerment. If it is difficult to contact "a part of yourself," sometimes we can make contact with someone in our past who gave us encouragement, letting his or her voice speak to us now.

3. Review the information gathered in steps one and two. Note your new learning in the space below.

4. If it seems appropriate, you may now wish to bring your new knowledge to bear on a current area in your life where you feel blocked. By focusing on the blocks with your awareness, you may begin the process of their dissolution. As we discover our capacity to expand beyond our imagined limitations, it becomes more possible for us to consider playing a part in our planet's survival.

Peace and Empowerment

We all have a treasure chest of guidance and nurturance within us. Our ways of contributing to peace will be as varied as ourselves. What is important is our common desire and ability to do so. When we begin to align ourselves with that power within ourselves, when we watch our fear and let it flap its wings without being immobilized by it, then we begin to walk the path of peace. We do not need millions of Gandhis to save the world. If we have millions of fully human, responsive individuals, connected through their love for the planet and its people, that will be enough.

SECTION VII: Spiritual Aspects of Building Peace

Repressing the Sublime

At one point during my planning of this manual, I had a session with my meditation teacher Sheila Krystal. Sheila had been instrumental in my deciding to write this manual, by suggesting that I contact an "inner guide" to aid in its creation. On this occasion, Sheila asked me how the manual was proceeding. I responded by listing all the sections I had included in my outline. "Is there anything you haven't included?" she asked. I closed my eyes, and began to associate. I imagined including "that which is not included" as a section of the manual. Sheila associated to the place setting left for Elijah at the Passover meal. Including the unseen guest. We then thought of the Sufi poet Kabir who refers to the Spirit as the Guest. At that point I became aware of a catch in my throat, and a flood of feelings and memories washed over me.

—I remembered the peace workshop I gave in Hamburg, where I announced that the workshop proper would continue the next morning at 9 a.m., and that I would be interested in discussing spiritual aspects of peace work with anyone who wished to do so at 8 a.m. At 8 a.m. all twenty group members appeared for the discussion.

—I remembered that in October 1983 I had coordinated and moderated a conference at U.C. Berkeley called, "Integrating Spirit and Society with Psychotherapy."

—I remembered a peace meditation that my sister and I had shared in Paris, the summer of '83.

—Most of all, I remembered with sadness how I had forgotten to include any specific reference to spiritual values in this manual.

Some transpersonal psychologists have coined the term, "repression of the sublime." I realize that I have done that to myself. I do not believe I am an exception. What may be unusual is how often I catch myself at it. On one hand, I wish to share with you and encourage you to develop and explore your spiritual insights and discoveries around the area of building peace; on the other hand, I hesitate to do so. I feel presumptuous and vulnerable talking about my relation to God, Unity, the Spirit, whatever you may call it. "You're neither a clergyman nor a guru, so where do you get off talking about spiritual matters?" . . . Thus speaks my judge. My response is: "My concern with the spiritual is a part of my humanness which I will not deny." To be concerned with all of humanity across time and space, to cherish humanity and to strive to protect and preserve it, brings my spiritual concerns into bold relief.

The Relevance of Spiritual Teachings

In the area of moral philosophy there is a statement, "virtue is its own reward." But we are still left with the question of what and who is virtuous. Many sects, nations, races, while fully believing in their own virtue, have slaughtered and oppressed others. Our present ability to extinguish all life on earth, forces us to take a more encompassing view of what is virtuous. The teachings of universal love and peace put forth by Jesus, Buddha, and others take on heightened meaning for those of us existing under the nuclear shadow. Awakening to these teachings can serve to sustain many of us who struggle in the shadow to bring peace to our planet.

So Many Paths

Each one of us has our own unique path to follow in this area. We come from so many different backgrounds: lapsed and devout Catholics; Orthodox, Reform and atheistic Jews; all sects and varieties of the Protestant faith; Muslims; Buddhists; Hindus; and Taoists. Some of us have thrown out the baby with the bathwater, and dropped spiritual concerns along with our parents' religion. Some of us are both religious and spiritual. We have studied with gurus, religious sects and teachers, and have been "burned." Others have been more or less enlightened. We are followers of non-gurus. Seekers and finders. Finders and losers. Others of us have come to our spiritual concerns through Tolstoy, Whitman, Blake, Hesse. Or through the example of people like Gandhi, King, Mother Theresa, E. K. Ross. There is such a banquet of spiritual choices open to many of us in the western world at this time. It is no wonder that thousands have suffered from spiritual indigestion, or simply have kept away from the table because the array seemed so bewildering. Indeed the analogy of a bazaar might be equally appropriate. Booths and stalls with each spiritual discipline hawking its wares. Some of us walk on, disgusted with the competitive tumult. At times it seems that all this din leads to confusion and despair.

EXERCISE 16: Contacting an Image of Spiritual Significance

So let's take a break from the banquet, the bazaar, the din and go back to our own image. Our image of peace.

Regain your center. With your feet feeling the earth, let that image of peace re-emerge for you. After staying with it for awhile, let it gently fade away. Invite your unconscious to now send you an image, a visual representation, or a symbol of spiritual significance for you. If it seems appropriate, you may choose to dialogue with it. Then come back into the here-and-now, feeling refreshed and relaxed. Whatever path you choose to take, your unconscious may be there with images and reminders to help you on your way. Record your visualization in the way you find most appropriate, in the space below.

My first spiritual image is that of the Lamed-Vav. Lamed-Vav is the number thirty-six in Hebrew. There is a legend going back through Jewish history about the thirty-six righteous ones. These individuals exist in every generation. No one, including themselves, knows who they are. What they do is what is important, not their individual glorification. These righteous ones are responsible for the ethical, moral, and even physical survival of the human race. Without them, the legend tells us, God would abandon us, and the Messiah would never come. As long as they exist, hope for our salvation remains. Quietly, without fanfare, the Lamed-Vav do their good works from one generation to the next.

The legend inspires me on several counts. My first association is to the power of good. We hear so much of the opposite on a daily basis. The media constantly bombard us with details of human greed, cruelty, and indifference. It seems impossible to maintain our hope for a better world in the face of such pervasive and powerful negative forces. Yet, here is this legend showing how a small number of people can make a great deal of difference. I think of them as the tiny grains of sand which transmute into a pearl. They provide a moral focus, a center around which others can rally, so that we all do not get swept into a moral vacuum. It is from the dark aridity of that vacuum that the possibility of planetary extinction has been hatched, and now slithers toward us all.

In the legend, each of the thirty-six live a life marked by discipline and commitment to the highest spiritual goals. Many have died across the generations, serving those goals and refusing to abandon them even in the face of the direst pressure.

So another spiritual lesson emerges, one having to do with dedication to the good within and without oneself. It seems that our present planetary context requires our spiritual stance to contain qualities inherent in both gold and iron. We need the beautiful soft gold of the loving compassionate heart, a golden love that encompasses all creation in a cherishing movement. Iron is also needed as part of our spiritual alchemy. Iron's strength and durability enable us to remain focused on our path towards internal and external peace despite the forces that seek to deter us.

Thus, a new image of spiritual significance has emerged for me. A bracelet of braided gold and iron. When I imagine wearing it, I think of the Lamed-Vav and all the countless, unknown others who have lived their lives heeding those inner voices that encourage compassion, peace, and understanding. My image of the golden-black bracelet inspires me to do the same.

Our spiritual images help link us to a source of power greater than any or all of us, a source within us all. Prayer is another way we can connect to that strength.

A Peace Prayer

Some prayers ask for a change in our internal state, others ask for a change in the external world. Still others are simply a way of expressing our joy and gratitude for being alive. I have found that praying for a desired internal change has often acted similarly to working with an affirmation. Praying has strengthened those qualities which I have wished strengthened. If it feels right for you, you may wish at this time or some later time, to offer a peace prayer. My offering is the following:

> I pray for the strength
> to keep on serving
> the planet and people,
>
> For the heart
> to allow in
> the suffering and the beauty,
>
> And for others
> to raise their voices
> in a song of peace.
>
> Amen.

SECTION VIII: Creating Your Peace Project

The act of creation is, in itself, a venture into the unknown. The creator of a peace project, idea, poem, or painting must be willing to go out on a limb. Courage and self-support are needed. We have often been rewarded for learning others' ideas, or following culturally dominant values. Most of us have not been encouraged to develop and manifest our own unique points of view. All too often, the opposite has been the case. Acknowledging the above helps us appreciate the potential for personal growth inherent in taking the risk of creating our own project for peace. The project becomes an opportunity for empowerment, a locus for stretching in ways you have not before.

Your project will be a unique extension of your resources, interests, and abilities. Think of yourself/your project as a wood carving in process. Before you shape it further, be aware of how the grain runs. See and feel the movement implicit in the present form; the movement which can be highlighted and made explicit with your help. Through self-awareness and reflection, the seed within can be brought into a full flowering. That flowering will be a gift not only to yourself, but also to all of us, and to the source which moves us to live and create. "More power to you," and when you feel ready, you can move on to the first step in this creative process.

Contemplating Your Resources

Any such project is a result of both inner and external forces. Turning inward, you can contemplate the areas in which you have shown interest, ability, and potential. Go back in time. Think of positive experiences where you utilized your strengths. Is it in the area of written communication? Artistic endeavor? Contacting people on a personal basis? Making things with your hands? Organizing or coordinating events? Touching people's hearts? Innovative ideas? Whatever category comes up for you can be part of your starting place. The other part is your social context. Will it be responsive to a project of this sort? Which people will tend to be most supportive, and how can you enlist whatever help you need?

This manual is one of my peace projects. It grew out of my 20 years of experience as a therapist, my experience with writing a few articles during the past years, my learning the value of right-brain experimentation, and my three years of work as peace activist.

My social context was highly supportive of this project. Both my men's group and my affinity group gave me much needed encouragement. I also had strong support from my wife and my circle of friends. This support was vital to my completing this manual.

EXERCISE 17: Taking Stock

Use the following blank space to record your inner and outer resources.

Now that you have done that part of the task using your left-brain abilities, we'll take the next step, which makes use of your right-brain potential.

EXERCISE 18: An Enabling Image

Ask for an image that will give you some general directions in which to move. Imagery is often like dreams. The message is delivered through metaphors and is not always immediately apparent. The meaning may become revealed as time passes. For instance, one morning I asked for an image related to creating a peace project. I followed the standard relaxation-imagery process, and the following story unfolded.

I see a deer in a forest. It is young and alone. I follow it through the woods. Finally it comes to a cabin. We enter, and find a young blond woman at work with a spinning wheel. I watch the spinning wheel spin, and think of wheels and spirals. I hear the spiritual: "Ezekiel saw the wheel away up in the middle of the air . . ."

A soft, colorful yarn is emerging from the wheel. Now I realize that there is another woman in the room. A middle-aged Native American who is at work with a loom. She is weaving the spun material into a bright cloth. The cloth can be used as a coat, decorative hanging, or rug. The work takes a long time. The deer patiently lies in the corner. Time passes and finally, the warm, colorful cloth is completed. I receive it as a gift, and leave the cabin. The deer, my guide, comes with me.

The message from my image is not direct. I'm not going to weave a poncho for peace. Yet, there is much there for me to ponder, to let deepen and bubble. I associate to various types of creative female energies, to the importance of duration, to the blending of the aesthetic and the useful, to the "give-away" gift I received. There are lessons here for me; there may be some for you also. Weeks later when I returned to this story, more meanings emerged.

Now you have the opportunity to allow your own unique image to emerge. When you feel ready, follow the relaxation and imagery process, and ask for an image, visual symbol or story, that will in some way help you in creating your own peace project. Begin.

EXERCISE 19: Visualizing Peace Project Guides

Each project/process has its beginning, middle, and end. The birthing process may be a long one. Bear with it, so to speak. Although inspiration and genesis may be very exciting; changing the diapers and weeding the field require another kind of energy.

I have tapped into my unconscious for specific guides to aid me in the various stages of creating this project. A glorious angel served as my inspirational muse; an earthy old man was my guide for the detail work that needed to be carried out, if this manual was to be brought out into the world.

When it feels like the right time for you, ask to meet and dialogue with whatever guides can help you in your endeavor. Be open to hearing from people in your life who may have offered guidance in the past or those who may have appeared in your dreams. A particular guide may appear as a voice, an animal, or a symbol. Note your interaction with your guide/s in the space below.

I remember when I first thought of writing this manual, I wasn't sure if I could carry out such an ambitious task. My guide, the earthy old man, didn't have much to say to me when I queried him regarding whether or not I should begin the project. He simply said, "write at least 15 minutes a day for a week; at the end of the week come back and see me." Excellent advice. I received the same advice the following week. By the time the two weeks had passed, I had written enough, and became involved enough, to realize that I was on my way.

Allow the Necessary Time

It's important to keep duration in mind as an integral part of creating this project. Music is a good example of the importance of duration. How long you keep a note going; how long you keep the silences between the notes is vital to the whole structure of the sound produced. If I were to make a graph of the energy I expended on this project over time, it would contain irregularly alternating peaks and valleys. It would be very uneven. The relatively little time I spent on the project before my big push in March 1984 was as vital as the big push itself. The plant does a lot of work under the ground before it finally pushes through in a relatively short time and begins to grow in the sun. Don't expect instant growth, instant productivity, instant project.

A Review of Creating Your Peace Project

Here's a final left-brain review of what to look for in creating your peace project. It falls under two major headings: Being Aware of Your Process; and Finding Guidance and Support.

I. Being Aware of Your Process
    A. Duration and Rhythm
        1. Be patient, allow for natural rhythms of creativity to be present.

    2. Realize that time, in and of itself, is often needed for something alive to develop and grow.

  B. Compassion vs. Criticality

    1. Be aware of how you approach new ideas and possibilities. Consider them lovingly, rather than dismissing them brusquely.

  C. Feeling Tone

    1. Be in touch with your general feeling tone as you do this project. Is it exciting or onerous? Do you experience yourself as learning and growing as you work on it?

II. Finding Guidance and Support

  A. From Yourself

    1. Find guided fantasies, images and stories that will serve as metaphors for your project and your process around your project.

    2. Meet specific guides through visualization for different parts of the project.

    3. Explore whatever combination of visualization, meditations, affirmations, and relaxation you can build around helping you to carry out this project. Refer back to section on Empowerment for more help in that area.

  B. From Others

    1. Encouragement: Get it from those likely to give it to you. It is an important ingredient to sustain you on what might be a risky or long path.

    2. Feedback: Be open to it. By letting the world in, and maintaining your center and focus, you can emerge with a synthesis that may have a greater impact on more people.

    3. Celebration: Allow yourself,the joy and feelings of well-being that come with carrying out a worthwhile task. Encourage others who have helped you to celebrate with you.

SECTION IX: Building Peace: What Will Sustain Us?

So here we are at the final turn of the spiral in this manual. The vertical axis has remained the same throughout: integrating the personal and political. Now, you may be ready to implement what you have learned, and start to carry out your peace project. However, carrying out a project is one thing, weaving peacemaking into the fabric of your life for years to come is another. I don't believe that peace will come either soon or precipitately. To render the nuclear threat obsolete may require the effort of millions over long periods of time. How, then, can we sustain the necessary personal-political effort to carry out this task? I believe that commitment, community, and co-creation can provide the energy needed to persevere in our endeavor.

Commitment

The word commitment often frightens us. We get images of either mental hospital inmates or fanatic true-believers. Commitment often seems synonymous with giving up an important part of oneself.

Many of my psychotherapy clients tell me of their fear of "being committed to a relationship." When questioned about the fear, they often equate commitment to a relationship with commitment to the other person. That commitment, they believe, means giving up their needs in order to satisfy the other. I have a different way of defining commitment. I consider myself deeply committed. Committed to that part of myself which I experience as loving, compassionate, and life-affirming. The part I would think of in spiritual terms as my "higher self." At first glance, self-commitment may appear selfish and narcissistic. However, the self I commit to is deeply aware of our interconnectedness and interdependence, and accepts that truth as a basis for building peace. This life-affirming self knows that cherishing the planet and people is a way of loving oneself; and cherishing oneself is another way of loving the planet and people. It knows that we are in win-win or lose-lose game. There is no longer space for win-lose. If we give to ourselves and ignore the rest of the world, our selfishness will contribute to our eventual isolation and misery. If we ignore ourselves and try to serve the world, we still won't find peace. By committing to that "higher self" within, we establish a win-win approach to the world and our lives. Using that commitment as a starting point, we can then move with clarity into the external world. Whether I am dealing with work, friendships, a love relation, or political issues, my focus remains the same. The question I ask myself is: Does this particular relationship or endeavor serve to enhance or weaken that part of myself?

When we begin to perceive our world in this manner, we have taken an important step towards guiding our own process of personal development. Now we have a goal, a compass, and a path to follow. Our goal is enhancement of our deepest personal potential. Our judgement, as to whether or not a particular activity or relationship furthers reaching that goal, serves as our compass. When we heed our judgement, we then follow the path of "right livelihood," or "an enriching relationship," and we move toward our goal.

Consider accepting my concept of self-commitment for yourself. Are you willing to commit yourself to the enhancement and development of those life-affirming parts you value the most? If you are, then you embark on a course rich in personal reward, requiring constant vigilance and effort. It is from that centered place that a self-sustaining approach to peace work can arise.

Working for peace will then be another way to fulfill your self-commitment. It will be a personal-political manifestation of your dedication to your higher self. If you are prepared to maintain this self-dedication throughout your life, then your peace work may become part of the ongoing fabric of your life in a congruent, natural way.

The nature of peace itself tends to elicit the best part of ourselves. When we think and work towards creating peace, we must immediately consider personal qualities such as compassion, understanding, and love. We also begin to think in terms of human interconnectedness and interdependence. This consciousness makes it harder for us to accede to tendencies towards isolation or domination. We wish to become part of a greater whole, and realize our unique role in that context rather than pulling away from or trying to control others. Thus, simply having peace be part of our consciousness on a regular basis can be an important catalyst for personal/spiritual development.

The process of working for peace may thus lead to the product of a more peaceful person, one more likely to be in touch with the parts of oneself that are of the highest value. Such a person can then be said to have achieved a personal-political integration around the core of commitment to their higher self. Commitment of this nature thus becomes a major sustaining force in continuing to work for peace.

Community and Co-creation

Building peace, as I have previously indicated, entails the ability to look unflinchingly into the face of the nuclear horror that threatens us all. We are thus put into the position of tightrope walkers, balanced precariously above a distant floor. On one side is the fall into pessimistic assumptions and paralyzing despair. On the other side, we can slip into denial and escapism. Either way, the result is inaction. We are both the acrobats and the safety net. By working for peace in community with others, we can support and be supported when we do slip.

Community can provide even more than this vital kind of support. Our mutual support can empower us to create new processes, projects, and concepts designed to take us further on the path towards peace. The international awakening of peace consciousness has manifested itself in countless ways. From a videotape about children's fear of nuclear holocaust to a giant home-made peace quilt; from a peace opera to a town declaring itself a nuclear-free-zone; from leaving peace pamphlets in an East Berlin church to protesting deployment of missiles in England. All these phenomena reveal the boundless creativity of the millions who wish to bring peace to the planet.

A great variety of groups form the context for this creative outpouring. Some of them are listed in the resource section of this manual. By finding or helping to start a co-creative peace community, you will be nourishing not only your wish to serve the planet, you will also be inspiring and enhancing your own creative potential. Cultivating these vital forces within you will add greatly to your ability to sustain a prolonged involvement in building peace.

A Next Step

There is a time for beginning and a time for ending. This is a time for both. You have nearly completed the manual. You now also have the opportunity to begin something new, to take a next step with your project, to explore your participation in a co-creative community, with the others who have read this manual. I suggest that all of you who are interested, send a short description of your project to *Awakening in the Nuclear Age Journal* (address in resource section). On a semi-annual basis, we will then mail back to you a list of projects carried out in your area. In this manner, you will be both inspired and a source of inspiration for others who are working to build peace.

In Closing

Give yourself an opportunity for savoring your completing this manual. You have devoted time and energy to this task. You may wish to close your eyes, and breathe deeply. Relax and feel the letting go. Allow memories, images, ideas to emerge for you as you recall your involvement with this manual. Be with them for as long as you wish, and then let go of those you wish to release. What needs to be retained, will be retained. Now let us close in gratefulness and appreciation for the gentle power within us all . . . The power to create a better, more peaceful world.

SECTION X: Resources

Resources Promoting Peace and Personal/Political Integration

I

Organizations and Networks

Interhelp
West Coast Office: 180 Andover Street
                      San Francisco, CA 94110
                      (415) 586-6311

National Office: P.O. Box 331
                  Northampton, MA 01061

This national/international network connects people who wish to work for peace utilizing their full human capacities. Branches exist in the U.K., Australia, New Zealand, Holland, Sweden, and West Germany.

Psychotherapists for Social Responsibility
P.O. Box 31346
San Francisco, CA 94131

An organization of mental health workers dedicated to raising consciousness about the planetary crisis.

Association for Humanistic Psychology
National Office: 325 Ninth Street
                  San Francisco, CA 94103

This international organization has recently made building peace one of its main concerns. The organization was initiated in 1960 by Carl Rogers, Rollo May, and Abraham Maslow among others.

II
Written Materials

Awakening in the Nuclear Age: A quarterly journal containing articles, poems, and reports relating to creating peace in an integrated way.

P.O. Box 4742
Berkeley, CA 94704
(415) 841-4545

Peace Resource Book, A Comprehensive Guide to Issues, Grants and Literature, Elizabeth Bernstein, Randall Forsberg, et al. Cambridge: Ballenger, 1986.

Capra, Fritjof, *The Turning Point*. New York: Simon and Schuster, 1982.
Hillesum, Etty, *An Interrupted Life*. New York: Pantheon Books, 1983.
Macy, Joanna, *Despair and Personal Power in the Nuclear Age*. Philadelphia: New Society Publishers, 1983.
Schell, Jonathan, "The Abolition: Defining the Great Predicament." *The New Yorker Magazine*, Jan. 1984.
Walsh, Roger, *Staying Alive*. Boulder: New Science Press, 1984.